SALMON

Printed in China

00 01 02 03 04 5 4 3 2 1

Library of Congress Cataloging-in-Publication Data
Baxter, John M., 1953-
Salmon / John M. Baxter
p. cm. — (WorldLife library)
Summary: Provides information about the main species of salmon, their evolution, life
cycles, migration, and threats to their existence, and more.
ISBN 0-89658-466-6 (alk. paper)
1. Salmon--Juvenile literature. [1. Salmon] I. Title. II. Series: World life library.
QL638.S2 B38   2000
597.5'6–dc21   99-089958
                                                                    CIP

Distributed in Canada by Raincoast Books, 8680 Cambie Street, Vancouver, B.C. V6P 6M9

Published by Voyageur Press, Inc.
123 North Second Street, P. O. Box 338, Stillwater, MN 55082 U.S.A.
651-430-2210, fax 651-430-2211

Educators, fundraisers, premium and gift buyers, publicists and marketing managers: Looking for creative products and new sales ideas? Voyageur Press books are available at special discounts when purchased in quantities, and special editions can be created to your specifications. For details contact the marketing department at 800-888-9653.

Photographs copyright © 2000 by

Front cover © Jeff Foott (BBC Natural History Unit)
Back cover © Laurie Campbell
Page 1 © Michael Quinton (Minden Pictures)
Page 3 © Paul Nicklen (Ursus Photography)
Page 4 © Jeff Foott (Auscape)
Page 6 © Harry M Walker
Page 8 © Sue Scott
Page 11 © Kennan Ward
Page 12 © Tom Walker (Planet Earth Pictures)
Page 15 © Michael Quinton (Minden Pictures)
Page 16 © Renée Kitt DeMartin
Page 19 © D. Parer & E. Parer-Cook (Auscape)
Page 20 © Renée Kitt DeMartin

Page 23 © Ken Sawada
Page 25 © Sue Scott
Page 26 © Paul Nicklen (Ursus Photography)
Page 29 © Bryan and Cherry Alexander
Page 30 © Jeff Foott (Auscape)
Page 33 © Hiromi Naito (Ursus Photography)
Page 34 © Jeff Foott (Bruce Coleman)
Page 36 © Art Wolfe
Page 37 © Jeff Foott (Bruce Coleman)
Page 38 © T Kitchin & V Hurst (NHPA)
Page 40 © Deni Brown (Oxford Scientific Films)
Page 43 © Ken Sawada
Page 44 © Kevin Schafer (NHPA)

Page 47 © Bryan & Cherry Alexander
Page 48 © Tom Walker (Planet Earth Pictures)
Page 51 © Kevin Schafer (NHPA)
Page 52 © Glyn Satterley
Page 55 © Laurie Campbell
Page 57 © Harry M Walker
Page 58 © John Shaw (Bruce Coleman)
Page 61 © Daniel J Cox (Oxford Scientific Films)
Page 62 © Laurie Campbell
Page 63 © Michael Roggo (Still Pictures)
Page 64 © David E Myers (Tony Stone Images)
Page 67 © Jeff Foott (Bruce Coleman)

SALMON

John M. Baxter

WORLDLIFE
LIBRARY

Voyageur Press

Contents

Introduction

Remarkable, awe-inspiring, mysterious: salmon are all of these and much more. In the North Atlantic the Atlantic salmon is supreme, with populations returning to rivers in many countries bordering the North Atlantic from Canada, Russia and Iceland in the north, to Scandinavia and the U.K., and as far south as Spain and Portugal. In the North Pacific there are six species of Pacific salmon that have various ranges from Japan and California in the south, to Arctic Russia and Alaska in the north.

Among the native peoples of many countries where salmon occur there are associated traditions, many of which stretch back into the mists of time. Without the salmon, the native peoples of the Pacific coastal regions could not have survived. They believed that only if the salmon were treated with respect would they continue to return. Thus rituals such as the 'First Salmon Ceremony' developed to pay tribute, and offer thanks to the salmon for returning yet again and ensuring the survival of the people.

On many parts of the coast of North America, people still practice the First Salmon Ceremony. Elsewhere, however, the ever-increasing pressures from the commercial exploitation of this valuable natural resource are demanding more and more of the sockeye and its cousins, which continue to return to their natal rivers year after year to spawn in their millions.

Similarly, the Atlantic salmon, often referred to as the 'King of Fish', is held in the highest esteem as both a valuable natural resource and a source of inspiration. Henry Williamson captured the essence of its life history in his saga *Salar the Salmon*. It has also been the subject of poetry and fiction, such as John Buchan's *John McNab*, and it is the substance of many apocryphal tales.

This book is a celebration of the salmon's majesty and their tragedy, and in some small way a tribute.

The classic image of a salmon in its relentless quest to reach the spawning grounds.

Salmon of the World

Salmon are members of one of the most primitive groups of bony fish. Modern-day salmon fall into two genera; *Salmo* – which includes the Atlantic salmon (*Salmo salar*), the brown trout, (*Salmo trutta*) and the rainbow trout (*Salmo gairdneri*) and *Oncorhynchus* – which includes the six species of Pacific salmon (chum salmon, *O. keta*; pink salmon, *O. gorbuscha*; sockeye salmon, *O. nerka*; chinook salmon, *O. tshawytscha*; coho salmon, *O. kisutch* and masu salmon, *O. masou*).

Pacific salmon and Atlantic salmon are sufficiently similar, both in appearance and ecological characteristics, that in the past there has been considerable debate as to whether they all belonged to a single genus or not. Although the distinguishing features that separate *Salmo* and *Oncorhynchus* are no longer in question they are undoubtedly closely related and their evolutionary sequence is well understood.

All seven species of salmon are to various degrees anadromous; that is, they undergo a migration from their natal freshwater river or lake out to sea, only to return to their freshwater origins to breed, and often to die. Within this basic life history, however, there are subtle variations in the timing of key events and habitat requirements of the different species.

It is generally assumed that the evolutionary ancestors of modern-day salmon were freshwater fish. The basic salmoniform fish is of great antiquity – at least 180 million years old. The Atlantic salmon is the most primitive and the various Pacific salmon have evolved, relatively rapidly, over the last six hundred thousand to one million years (during the Pleistocene epoch) from an ancestral Atlantic salmon stock. Towards the end of the Pliocene, around two million years ago, the Pacific and Atlantic Oceans were connected across what is the present Arctic region. This connection is borne out by the presence of many animal species in both the Pacific and Atlantic Oceans, but not so for *Oncorhynchus* and *Salmo*. This connection was then lost and throughout the Pleistocene, despite fluctuating sea levels due to advancing and retreating ice ages, it was never re-established.

Journey's end. An Atlantic salmon at the headwaters of the River Avon, Scotland.

As with all evolutionary history we can only speculate on what actually occurred but it would seem that the initial separation of the stocks of *Oncorhynchus* from the ancestral *Salmo* took place not later than the early Pleistocene.

In and around the indented coastline of the Asiatic margins of the Pacific Ocean, large areas of enclosed brackish waters formed as a result of land and sea level changes. In these isolated water masses, rapid evolution of species occurred and it is here, probably in what is now the Sea of Japan, that the evolution from a far-flung stock of *Salmo* into *Oncorhynchus* began. With the reconnection of the enclosed waters of the Sea of Japan to the rest of the Pacific Ocean, this new, distinct stock, whether or not as yet a fully-fledged genus, was able to extend its range. Throughout the Pleistocene there were repeated appearances and disappearances of land and ice barriers in the North Pacific. These barriers resulted in the creation of other isolated bodies of water that persisted for anything between 50,000 and 100,000 years. Within these waters *Oncorhynchus* underwent further divergences, creating the different species that we see today.

The evolutionary history of Pacific salmon can be traced based on ecological, physiological and biochemical characteristics. The masu salmon is the most primitive and closely related to the Atlantic salmon; it is largely confined to coastal waters around the Sea of Japan. It is believed that some male masu salmon that mature in fresh water survive after spawning. The other five species show varying degrees of divergence: the chinook and coho salmon have marked similarities and remain quite distinct from pink and chum salmon which are themselves closely related. Physiological and behavioral similarities between pink and chum salmon, suggest that the two species diverged relatively recently in the evolutionary timescale. The sockeye salmon is the most distinct species and occupies an intermediate evolutionary position between the chinook/coho pairing and the pink/chum pairing.

Chum salmon *Oncorhynchus keta*

The name 'keta' is derived from the language of the Nanai people who live in the Khabarovsk and Primore regions of Russia, and literally means 'fish'.

Iridescent scales on the flank of a chinook salmon.

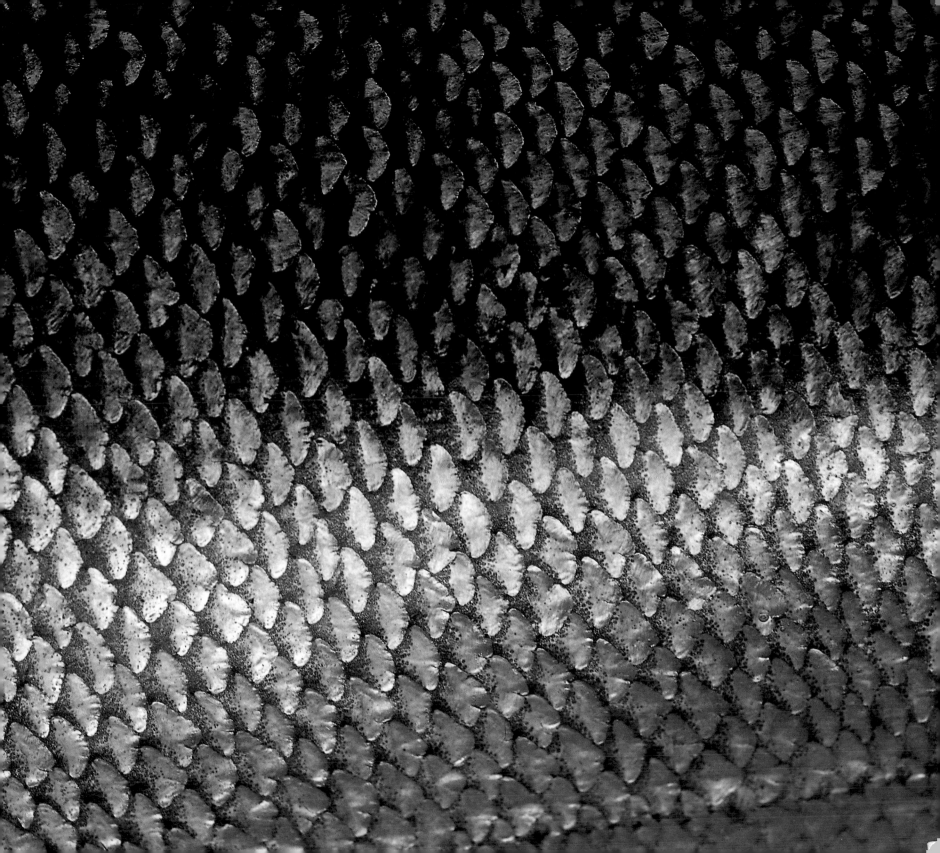

*Chum salmon in full spawning livery and displaying the large
canine-like teeth that earn them the vernacular name 'dog salmon'.*

The young fry have a green iridescence on their back with a series of slender, vertical bars (or parr marks) that extend only slightly below the lateral line. Adult fish can grow up to 43 in (109 cm) in length, and weigh as much as 44 lb (20 kg), although more typically they reach around 26–30 in (66–76 cm) and 9–13 lb (4–6 kg). They have a striking metallic-blue dorsal surface with occasional black speckling, the flanks are silver and all but the dorsal fin have distinctive dark tips. In fresh water maturing fish lose their metallic-blue sheen for a dullish green, and develop dark reddish streaks and pale blotches on their flanks, together with white tips to the pelvic and anal fins. Mature male fish develop large, canine-like teeth earning them the vernacular name 'dog salmon'. In Canada and the U.S.A. they are also known as the calico salmon, while in Russia and Japan there are many other regional names.

Chum salmon have the widest geographic distribution of all the Pacific salmon. They spawn in rivers stretching from north California through Oregon, Washington State, British Columbia and Alaska. In Arctic Alaska they are found in the Arctic Red and Peel Rivers, tributaries to the great Mackenzie River, and in the Slave and Hay Rivers that flow through the Great Slave Lake. On the Asian coast they occur as far south as Honshu through the Sea of Okhotsk, the Kamchatka Peninsula and Anadyr Bay to the Kolyma and Lena Rivers in Arctic Siberia. During their sea phase, chum salmon are distributed throughout the North Pacific above around 46°N and into the Bering Sea.

In years when there are large numbers of chum salmon the mean size of returning adults decreases, while the age of these mature fish increases. There is also marked competition between young chum and pink salmon: when young pink salmon are abundant, the survival rate of young chum salmon in coastal waters is lower; this pattern persists in the oceanic phase of their life. Conversely, during years when pink salmon numbers are lower, there are larger numbers of chum salmon.

Pink salmon *Oncorhynchus gorbuscha*
The fry of pink salmon are bluish-green along their back with silvery flanks and without any other markings. The adults are striking fish with an iridescent metallic-blue dorsal surface, silver sides and an opalescent white belly. The back, upper sides and caudal fin all bear

numerous large, black, almost oval spots. Mature males change in appearance, developing a very pronounced hump immediately behind the head and growing a distinct downward-pointing hook on the upper jaw. This change in shape has earned them the vernacular name of the humpback salmon. There is also a marked color change, with mature males developing red and yellow blotches on their sides and a general darkening on their back. The females undergo a similar change in coloration.

The pink salmon has a very large geographic spread; in British Columbia alone it is estimated that there are around 2200 separate spawning stocks. Pink salmon are found in the Sea of Japan from around the coast of Hokkaido, Japan, and the Tumen River, at the border between North Korea and Russia, extending northwards throughout the Sea of Okhotsk and Sakhalin Island, the Kamchatka Peninsula, the Bering Sea and the northern coast of Russia as far east as the Yana and Lena Rivers which flow into the Arctic Ocean. On the North American coast they extend from central California northwards around the coast, including the Aleutian Islands and reportedly as far east as the Mackenzie River in Arctic Canada, although recent surveys have not recorded any pink salmon from this system. The majority of the spawning stocks are confined to a band between 45°N and 65°N on both continents.

Pink salmon are the most numerous of the Pacific salmon species. In recent years the total annual commercial catch has been around 160 million fish, with west and east coast fisheries accounting for roughly 50 per cent each, the majority being caught by fisheries in the U.S.A. and Russia.

The pink salmon is the smallest of the Pacific salmon, typically reaching between 18 and 22 in (46 and 56 cm) in length and weighing between 3 and 5 lb (1.4 and 2.3 kg). A few pink salmon weighing up to 12 lb (5.4 kg) have been recorded but these are very much the exception. Pink salmon have a rigid two-year life-cycle and in many rivers and streams there is a two-year cycle of dominance, with either odd or even years consistently having much larger runs of fish.

The female pink salmon excavates the nest while the attendant male lies alongside.

Sockeye salmon *Oncorhynchus nerka*

Sockeye is a corruption of the name used by the native peoples of southern British Columbia – 'sukkai' – and its variants in the dialects of the Sooke, Snohomish, Comox, Saanich, Musqueam and Chilliwack. It is also known by other names in its range, including red salmon in Alaska, blueback salmon along the Columbia River, 'nerka' in Russia and 'benizake' or 'benimasu' in Japan. In addition to the vast numbers that migrate to sea each year there are also non-anadromous populations found in many lake systems. These are known as 'kokanee'.

Sockeye fry have an iridescent green, unmottled back with silver flanks and a white underside. A series of vertical dark parr marks run along each side extending only a short distance below the lateral line. The adult fish have a beautiful greenish-blue back with sparsely distributed fine black speckles. The flanks are brilliant silver. Maturing fish change color, in both sexes the head becomes olive green, the back and sides bright red, shading to darker red with green and yellow blotches more ventrally and white on the ventral surface. The male also changes shape, becoming laterally compressed and developing a pronounced fleshy hump in front of the dorsal fin.

The main sockeye spawning stocks have a relatively restricted range, due to their dependence on lakes for spawning and the initial growth of their young. On the North American coast they occur from around the Sacramento River in California to Kotzebue Sound. The main concentrations are found in the Bristol Bay watershed and the Fraser River drainage system of British Columbia, together with other systems such as the Skeena, Nass and Somass Rivers. On the Asian coast the main distribution is confined to around the Kamchatka Peninsula up as far north as the Anadyr River. Small numbers, however, are found as far north as Cape Chaplina and as far south as the north coast of Hokkaido and the Okhota and Kukhtoy Rivers, on the north-west coast of the Sea of Okhotsk in Russia.

In recent years catches of sockeye salmon have been in excess of 60 million fish, the majority being caught by Alaskan and British Columbian fisheries. Sockeye salmon flesh is darker red than other species, making it particularly appealing to the canning industry. Sockeye

A mature male sockeye salmon at the spawning grounds.

salmon vary in size depending on their river of origin. Fish from the Columbia River average only 3½ lb (1.6 kg), whereas those from the Fraser River average 6 lb (2.7 kg) and the largest are found in the Chignick River on the Alaska Peninsula, averaging 7 lb (3.2 kg).

Chinook salmon *Oncorhynchus tshawytscha*

The chinook salmon is also known as the spring salmon, king salmon or tyee (the Chinook word for 'large'); returning fish typically weigh up to 44 lb (20 kg). Fish of 99 lb (45 kg) are not uncommon and even larger fish are occasionally caught, such as a 126 lb (57 kg) fish measuring 53 in (135 cm) in length recorded in Petersburg, Alaska. There is an unofficial record of a fish weighing over 134 lb (61 kg).

Chinook fry have large, vertical, dark marks that extend well below the lateral line; the adipose fin (the small fleshy fin between the dorsal fin and the tail) is unpigmented except for a striking dark tip. Markings are, however, variable. Adult fish are greenish-blue on their dorsal surface mottled with large, irregular black spots that extend to the dorsal and caudal fins. In fresh water the maturing fish take on a dull dark greenish-bronze color. Uniquely, the adult chinook salmon has variable flesh color, from white through shades of pink to red, the color associated with all other salmon.

The chinook salmon is the least numerous of the five species of Pacific salmon that occur along the North American coast. Numbers have been declining steadily over many years, resulting in very low numbers in the mid 1980s, and although locally in some places stocks are gradually increasing, in many river systems spawning populations are still under serious threat.

There are around 1500 spawning populations of chinook salmon, the majority along the North American coast extending from the San Joaquim/Sacramento River system in California throughout the Aleutians and as far north as the Yukon River in Alaska. There are some, as yet unconfirmed, reports of chinook salmon in the Fraser and Coppermine Rivers in the Canadian Arctic. On the Asian coast spawning stocks are found from northern Hokkaido, all around the coast of the Sea of Okhotsk and the Bering Sea as far north as the Anadyr River.

Most of the spawning populations are small and potentially vulnerable to over-exploitation, and only a few, such as those in western Kamchatka, remain unexploited. Many

*An increasingly rare sight. The numbers of chinook salmon continue
to decline on most rivers and on many urgent action is needed to reverse this trend.*

spawning populations are estimated at less than 1000 spawners, but a few, particularly those at the extremes of the range, are much larger. On the Yukon and Nushagak Rivers, runs of between 400,000 and 600,000 regularly occur. The chinook salmon is the ultimate prize fish for anglers due to its large size. Approximately one million are caught each year in sports fisheries.

Coho salmon *Oncorhynchus kisutch*

The coho fry is a dull-gold color with around 11 narrow dark-brown parr marks on either side that extend equally above and below the lateral line. The fins are orange and the anal fin has a white leading edge with a parallel dark stripe. As the fry change into smolts (the stage at which salmon migrate from fresh water to the sea, somewhere between one and three years of age) they become more silvery, the fins change to a pale yellow and the dorsal surface takes on a greenish-blue tinge. Adult sea-going fish have a striking dark metallic-blue dorsal surface with irregular black spots, silvery flanks and ventral surface. As the fish mature on their return to fresh water, they undergo a dramatic transformation, with males changing to bright red, with a contrasting bright-green head and back, and a dark belly. The females take on a similar pattern but are much less strongly colored. In males the upper jaw forms an elongated hooked snout that may grow so large as to prevent the mouth from closing.

Adult fish average between 6 lb and 12 lb (2.7–5.4 kg), reaching around 22–26 inches (56–66 cm) in length; fish over 20 lb (9 kg) are rare and the heaviest ever recorded was a 31 lb (14 kg) fish caught off Victoria, British Columbia, in 1947.

Coho salmon return to many rivers and streams on the west coast of North America, from the San Lorenzo River north to Kotzebue Sound and Point Hope in Alaska. Their main centre of abundance is between Oregon and south-east Alaska. They are found scattered throughout the Aleutian Islands but have only a patchy distribution along the Asian coast where they are found in the Anadyr River, the southern regions of Kamchatka, the Sea of Okhotsk, Sakhalin, northern Hokkaido and Peter the Great Bay in Korea.

Throughout its range numbers are declining and some small spawning stocks are under

The perpetuation of the stock depends on these coho salmon successfully spawning.

threat of extinction. Coho salmon are a favorite of anglers, who account for a significant proportion of the total annual catch, which in recent years has been less than 20,000 tonnes.

Masu salmon *Oncorhynchus masou*

Masu salmon fry are a pale golden color, with a darker back mottled with bold black dots, and a series of vertical parr marks equidistant above and below the lateral line, which has a reddish tinge. The dorsal, pelvic and anal fins are tipped with white. The adult masu salmon have a steely black back, grading through silver flanks to a white belly. As mature masu return and enter their natal rivers their appearance changes; body color darkens and they develop a pattern of orange-red and olive markings. The upper and lower jaws of the male fish become hooked.

Masu are restricted to the Asian coast of the North Pacific. They are found from the south-eastern tip of Korea and Honshu up through Hokkaido, from Sakhalen to the Amur River in Russia and around the coast of western Kamchatka. The status of stocks throughout its range is not well documented. It is, however, a valuable fish although it accounts for only about 2.5 per cent (4000 tonnes) of the total catch of salmon by the Japanese fisheries. Adult fish average around 5½ lb (2.5 kg) in weight when they return to their natal rivers to spawn.

Atlantic salmon *Salmo salar*

The Atlantic salmon gained its name *Salmo*, which means 'the leaper', from the Romans, who encountered it in many of the rivers of northern Europe as they marched northwards almost 2000 years ago. The Atlantic salmon is known as the 'King of Fish' and has long been the prized quarry of both commercial netsmen and anglers.

Atlantic salmon parr have a silvery body with a row of parr marks like grayish-blue thumbprints along the body, straddling the lateral line, with a red spot between each. The back may also be dotted with brown or black spots, and the leading edge of the pectoral and pelvic fins is white.

When adult fish return from the sea they have dazzling silver sides and a silvery-white belly, and their back may be olive-green to dark blue. The greatest prize for any angler is to

Salmon are a prized catch for anglers around the world, regardless of whether
they are the mighty chinook, spring-run Atlantic salmon or this small stream-type masu salmon.

catch a salmon soon after it has entered the river, and it can receive no higher accolade than to be revered as 'a bar of silver'. As they mature in the river prior to spawning, the silver fades and they take on a bronze-pink color. Cock fish may darken further with time to a mottled pattern of brown, red and purple, often with red spots – an appearance that leads to the most colored fish often being referred to as 'tartan fish'. The lower jaw of the cock fish also develops a pronounced hook or 'kype' and the whole skull elongates. As females mature they too lose the silver color, taking on a dull purplish sheen with red spots.

Unlike Pacific salmon, some Atlantic salmon survive after spawning, reverting to a silvery appearance, but are rather thin and flaccid. These fish are known as kelts and some manage to return to the sea where they regain their condition, before migrating again to spawn.

Atlantic salmon average between 23½ in and 29½ in (60 and 75 cm) in length and weigh 6–10 lb (2.7–4.5 kg). Salmon that have spent only one winter at sea before returning to spawn are known as grilse and may weigh as little as 2 lb (0.9 kg). Some fish may weigh up to 48½ lb (22 kg), but these are increasingly rare (fish in excess of 22 lb (10 kg) are considered large). The record for a rod-caught salmon in Scotland is 64 lb (29 kg). The world record is held by a 79 lb (36 kg) fish caught in Norway in 1925.

Atlantic salmon occur on the east coast of North America as far south as the coast of Massachusetts but only in very low numbers. They occur along the entire coast of Newfoundland, extending north through Labrador. The Kapisigdlit River is the only river in Greenland that has a salmon spawning population. Iceland and the Faroe Islands support numerous spawning populations. Atlantic salmon occur as far south as the coast of Portugal and Spain and extend northwards including the Baltic Sea coast and the U.K., reaching their north-eastern limit in the Pechora River in Russia which empties into the Barents Sea.

Catch figures have shown a steady decline over the last 25 years, although in recent years this has been due in part to a reduction in fishing effort. In 1998, the reported total global catch of Atlantic salmon was 2401 tonnes.

Atlantic salmon stocks are showing serious signs of decline with fewer
and fewer returning to spawn each year. In some places they are already locally extinct.